HARRY GUEST · SOME TIMES

Also by Harry Guest

HARRY GUEST

Some Times

Anvil Press Poetry

Published in 2010
by Anvil Press Poetry Ltd
Neptune House 70 Royal Hill London SE10 8RF
www.anvilpresspoetry.com

This book is published with financial assistance
from Arts Council England

Designed and set in Monotype Ehrhardt by Anvil
Printed and bound in Great Britain
by Hobbs the Printers Ltd

ISBN 978 0 85646 425 6

A catalogue record for this book
is available from the British Library

for Peter Jay

ACKNOWLEDGEMENTS

Grateful acknowledgement is due to publications in which some of the following poems have appeared:

Dealings with the Real World, Smith/Doorstop, 1987; *The New Exeter Book of Riddles* edited by Kevin Crossley-Holland and Lawrence Sail, Enitharmon, 1999; *Full of Star's Dreaming*, a tribute to Peter Redgrove, Stride, 2003; *The Review of Contemporary Poetry* edited by Gary Bills, bluechrome, 2005; and *The Lie of the Land* edited by Jan Fortune-Wood, Cinnamon Press, 2006

Also *Agenda*, *Dorset Echo*, *Fire*, *HQ Poetry*, *Jacket*, *The London Magazine*, *Magma*, *The North*, *Oasis*, *Otter*, *PN Review*, *Poetry Wales*, *Quattrocento*, *The Rialto*, *Shearsman*, *South West Review* and *Stand*.

CONTENTS

Those Days

Tho' much is taken, much abides
– TENNYSON

The Custard Mountains

A burst of atmospherics like
black sparks of sound flecked the suave Third
Programme voice. I'd lugged my sister's
heavy blue wireless upstairs. Gales
scraping The North Sea dashed salt rain
against the panes. The boy I used
to be had just heard of Lorca.
That week's Radio Times promised
half an hour of his poems read
in English. My obedient ear
managed to trace 'a line of light'
drawn above 'the custard mountains'.
I saw them vividly as heaped
and treacherous – a quaking ridge
whose sheen and softness must have lured
unwary pilgrims to their high
yellow horizon. Did they sink?
Could they return? What lay beyond?
Maybe a sulphur plateau? Lakes
of liquid gold? Or a forest
with foliage of saffron flame?
No spurts of image mattered since
that shiny dollop of a range
existed in a poet's mind
and was its own conviction – not
only that time listening alone
to words in my cold bedroom but
as fodder for bewildered dreams.
The printed page years later proved
how he'd limned a sky of Spanish
brilliance to form a backdrop
for some 'clustered mountains' and those
vulnerable lemon–coloured
mirages vanished for ever.

Limnads

I saw one once or rather
salvaged a glimpse of pale grey
sorrow just as mist at dusk
drifted on the pewter-dull
sheen of a pool not quite up
to being labelled a lake
oval-shaped some thirty feet
across at its widest point
not fed by any trickle
I could hear half-concealed by
willows in their autumn state
unstirred that evening by wind

She it surely must have been
like her cousins Apollo
hires to keep birchwoods from harm
guard springs frequent gaunt uplands
watch over brooks she must tend
that place with melancholy
not warding off casual
wayfarers although no paths
lead there but unwilling or
unable to offer some
form of welcome shies away
from contact with immortals
also and wanders daylong
nightlong round her appointed
area unsinging formed
of haze and uncertainty
though dutiful like all her
replicas in charge of still
meres disused canals dark ponds
hard to locate preferring
overcast skies in steady

mourning for the unreturned
careful no tear of theirs should
dent an unruffled surface
anywhere standing waters
allow a blurred mirroring
of moon or sundisc only
to let it go again with
no sense of loss no regret
just quiet grief waiting for
nothing to occur once more

Delayed Response

'Ronsard me celebroit'

I like at times to picture one
turned seventy like me now who'll
scan with weak eyes a poem that
hints gaily at our goings-on
then slipping present whereabouts
go back to see us lying there
lit by a fading afternoon
limned in few phrases frank enough
to mince a matter of such worth
to me still and perhaps to you
or do I prop up hope in vain
because you may no longer have
a book of mine to pluck down from
some dusty shelf though if you do
may I maybe beyond the grave
imagine a remembered smile
curving those lips which did so much
to please my body in those months
long over spent in outlawry
and unrepeatable except
in closely guarded metaphors
to fête your springtime pledged to my
October so I wonder now
will that greyed future self repay
with interest my gratitude
by conjuring up a rueful 'yes
that's how it was when I was young
and he was keen on me' before
closing the telltale page you check
your watch against the calendar
and turn away forever from
mementoes of a time mislaid

Dawn Redwood

Identify a starlet from the late
'40s pouting alongside Nicholas
Mimosa in a wrongly neglected
noir. Those slats. The intermittent neon.
Why was that Pontiac parked on a wet
street with a dead woman at the wheel? Cut
to a dark cactus dominating that
glassed-in porch as a gloved hand tries the door.
Ice-box begins to hum on the sound-track.
Phone dangling and an anxious voice Hello?
Hello? Or maybe a bleak image shot
sumptuously by Ansel Adams in
say Wyoming – tall spiky silhouette
glossily blackened against a silver
sky where massive clouds are flattened above
its rippled reflection on a lake. No.
A Chinese farmer on a limestone bluff
saw with awe a tree thought lost for ever
left over from prehistory like some
arboreal coelacanth in the same
decade. Father in triumph ringed the word
'extinct' in the Shorter Oxford. *Having*
a hollow spine. 'Akantha' means thistle,
thorn, one of a porcupine's needles or
a herring's backbone. A cartoon in *Punch*
had a fishmonger asking 'Coelacanth
or haddock, madam?' cheapening I suppose
the wonder. Nowadays they've grown several
healthy specimens from seeds gone missing
for millennia. Dawn Redwood. Someone
who knows? may some day catch his breath as he
sees the striped shadow of a sabre-toothed
tiger pad past a clump of fossil trees.

As Far as Angkor Wat

counts comma it might seem one writing life
is done with once we've reached the place where what
astounds anew dash old complexities
arising from a blurred reaction to
some given scene resembling cloudlight on
a ruin or four buffaloes getting rinsed
in a brown river dash had after all
its origin in humid aerodromes
at midnight in southeastern portions of
the atlas waiting with the children for
the next Dakota colon where with stars
gone soft above or noon trampling on shadows
can data be unearthed to rectify
a theme gone suspect question mark what if
the in inverted commas schedule planned
to test interpretations of the lost
finds references on from then to now
and later shaken down to only one
conclusion question mark dreams have their own
vocabulary comma designate
another truth each time pointing the gaze
in cycles to a stale experience
full stop close survey may provide distilled
interrogation of the motive like
a sandstone avatar or mango branch
the way a moat now grazed by oxen rings
a site arrived at after years of longing
dash journals pored over tired in twilight since
the artist armed with bias saunters out
plundering what communities of faith
built for to forge subjective patterns which
convey all the same elegies full stop
bird cries now echo into silence round

grey basreliefs and sunsplit courtyards till
eventual proportions start to curdle
about the involving I making the new
unknown a newer memory full stop
what's been derived from yellowed pamphlets helps
only in part dash even photographs
must cheat because you have to pace the thing
out for yourselves and sense uneven steps
comma a mediaeval play of sun
down far symmetric cloisters comma see
firsthand the blackening waste of rain along
those crumbling arcades full stop at first
not even pillagers full stop the splendour
went unremembered if at times huntsmen
intent on shooting monkeys down from trees
rooted in towers stumbled across paved floors
laid in oblivion and failed to find
some boles too angular dash otherwise
between haphazard expeditions only
the scrape of cobras over brickwork comma
a leopard's cough and the perpetual shove
of vegetation through the cracks full stop
ah may the ashes of forgotten sculptors
windswept arrange a spectral advocate
to arraign the gods they chiselled and produce
the battered finery as proof although
each statue hides a secret with its smile
because the done is still the thing which counts
comma response to problems of technique
which argues setting up against the murk
a witness to the self though self is doomed
full stop peripheries of anguish where
a limited hand cuts one crisp lintel full
of dancers comma legends comma flowers
may well exclude the stellar order or
conceal the desolation comma fear

of failure comma nothing rounded off
full stop lianas of the passing night
scrawl commentaries on what has been achieved
but cannot mask a proven impetus
nor punctuate an unspelt myth full stop

Duloe

for Penelope Shuttle

A blurred photo black and white
with my thumb in one corner
didn't at the time catch nor
can it even now retain
wonder at the way life chose
to start in that site so long
out of use although the tall
monoliths of quartz set by
dead strangers in a flattened
circle carried on sparkling
in spite of an April sun
stubbornly shrouded above
the place where a cow had just
calved for as I approached I
saw the afterbirth hanging
as a great transparent bag
near the red yard of her end
of the cord and the newborn
curled on the turf its mother
licking it but I felt there
ought to have been a sudden
fall of sunlight to alter
colour in the grass laying
dark shadows to make sure each
of the stones stayed steady till
the calf could totter up on
to uncertain hooves and find
a teat to be nuzzling while
yellow springshine warmed its flanks
in welcome to a world where
meaning seems to have need of
an arbitrary link between

one ragged field and the lost
motives of prehistory far
simpler than mere witnessing
though easier as always
to set down than decipher

Dream City

It kept on being me
sometimes as frightened schoolboy
then all at once myself as almost now
flustered, finding a familiar street
then blundering across an unknown square
among a throng who didn't speak my language.

I'd lost the others
whoever they were
having stopped to tie my shoelace
in the suddenness of an unsuspected space
before a rococo church

What I was seeing lay ahead
but then I watched my hurrying figure in longshot
seen it seemed from a high building

Reaching the port
panting, damp with sweat,
I fumbled out passport and ticket.

They refused to believe who I am

The siren blew
I rushed past, put a foot on the gangplank
got hauled back screaming protests
stood helpless on the quay
as the good ship *Esperance* left the harbour

Palindrome: The Loire Valley

Blue glow of tapestries: twisting leaves
and fountains of fabric surround Paris
choosing unwisely with a woven apple.
Along the lazy river-curve two boys
in boxer's shorts carry their fishing-rods
laterally like spears. In the low château
marquises stand flattened in gilt frames,
bewigged or bearded, togged in iron or velvet,
each crest sable flory with a daystar or.
Explosion from the quarry: beyond
the regular greygreen of poplars
a puff of stone-dust makes an amber fog.
Pods of the broom are swayed, Plantagenet,
the lovers' flower dragged through wounds
for a hundred years. Khaki jet-planes
slant in formation across the sky, a hand's-
breadth sooner than the noise they cause.
Kings pace whispering cobbles pursued
by regents, toadies, the curse of their victims,
hissing of treaties and sieges, meaning nothing
to me who rather heeded the curve of lips
pouting at sunlight from the desk next to mine.
Hunched shapes on motor-bikes roar round a camp-site,
faces hidden by plastic visors. The dragon
hovers by a slim tower while kilted peasants,
unconcerned, prune vines – they'd always thought
that bride the count brought home a trifle odd.
It costs a franc to phone and when you overrun
a light starts pulsing till you shove more coins in
to ask how the children are faring. On the frail
balcony, ladies, wimpled, gossiping,
watched a mock war on the parched sloping lawn
effete now with petunias. Too many names cut

on the memorial of the smallest village –
'the flower of France' untraceable in gas or mud.
Aquatic images flicker on the ceiling,
the moat is clogged, but we can hear the scrape
of quill on vellum as the poet writes yet again
for cash. Lorries judder by, all day, all night,
bringing crops before season. A suit of armour
leans from its niche, anonymous, beaked casque
flaunting plumes above slits for eyes.
The Tricolore droops at noon and newly-weds
come out of the Mairie hand in hand
to begin married life as a photograph.
Each arch of the bridge forms a perfect oval
and elms obey their own reflection as blurred
swifts scream and wheel high over plunging clouds.
Old enemies park next to each other, nod and frown
when told of conflicts or reprisals, doing
a right turn in unison when the guide
points to the captured flag. The mason knew
where bunches of grapes tangled with barley-sheaves
hid in the creamy block of tufa. In field
after field the sunflowers face two hours behind
summer's altered time. After the tourney
the luckier knight handed the lance to his squire –
the tall blade slants now in a whitewashed corner
draped with pale ribbon near a neat inked label.
We drive to our hotel past hoardings advising
a foreigner whom to vote for, explaining
why banks love to dish out money, proving
how hair-spray makes a goddess, offering
sly tips for the timeliest bargains
and prophesying when each one of us
will get the golden fruit that is our due.

Le Lion d'Angers, 1984

Mysteries of Old Age

for Phyllis

She doesn't actually miss her sister
only
after sixteen years in the same house
there's something wrong about each day

Although she's deaf
(a casual touch when her back's turned
causes unwelcome surprise)
she'll stop on the way to a favourite chair
and stare for some time at a spot
where there is
                    (apparently)
                                nothing to be seen

The world outside no longer tempts her
neither a neighbour's orchard
nor our backyard under buddleia
but she has been known to look
        puzzled and wistful
at a once familiar windowsill

There are grumpy moments
also unexplained skitterings
yet she needs more than ever
to be the centre of attention
(when of course it suits her)

Stiffer in the limbs now
it takes her just a little longer
to settle in my lap – there'll be
a querulous implication I should shift

and then another paw to be cleaned
before she curls into a half-circle
blinks faintly puzzled up at me
and begins to purr

Unnatural History

I can remember much forgetfulness.
— HART CRANE

It could be fiction told by another. Voice
mellifluous in my ear. Not like
pulse-echoes sleepless on the pillow.
You long ago, say, lying with me here –
this scoop of turf high up, reached
scrambling through wet bracken. Wales
a blur to the west where, then seventeen,
I, pointing, told you I'd been born. 'Oh?'
Uninterested nod before we kissed. Is that
what I have limped five miles to re-assess?
Standing in to-day's wind to smell
the oncoming rain. Pre-Cambrian evidence
breaks here and there the green. We chose to store
each imprint of our privacy where Iron
Age farmers threw up their defences.
Now seventy I don't intend to lie –
not even briefly – on damp ground. Ah, then
it burned with summer. You though blond
were tanned. Sunlight became you. We met
five times. I stammered my suggestion but
the choice of place got left to you. 'Here.'
And you stabbed the map. I peered at wavering
contours, unsure what to expect. My
inexperience – naïvety – call
it what you will – sparred blindfold
with that would-be guilt of yours. Martins,
white-bellied, swoop, veer as
unpredictably, making no sound.
What did I want of you more or less
than all we then did together? Although
by no means all. Queries unuttered

torn by this hasty autumn air. Despite
the programme cowering behind your eyes
I failed unflustered to de-code those suave
presuppositions. Older than you
I ought in theory to have wrested
total control. Not lie contented
with bewilderment as you slid round
between my arms. But is that how it was?
I'll never know even after winter's laid
one sterile colour on these hills. To have
taken your wrist less gently, led
you down a track in chiaroscuro where now
in mid-September lords-and-ladies stud
the wood's half-light with orange lanterns. Down,
then, down, shadowed by evergreens, to a chained
gate, weather-beaten, guarding an untilled field –
one governed by a different slant of sun.
My fault we stayed so unadventurous
an hour or more each time above the plain.
Since one of us apparently preferred
blank interruption to remorse. I move off
along the grass rampart, notice – shaking,
delicate – five pale mauve harebells
in a dip where we may have been lying.
I can't pretend I recognise the place.
After so long. Nor see what I had missed. I touch
each flower, pick one. Hearing across the decades
no murmured pledges from our times together.
We left, caressed by longing. Bared torso.
Ruffled hair. In triumph? Well, who can tell –
not I now, certainly. Nor you,
unfindable as fingerposts to a lost July.
I haven't brought the camera. There might
have been elusive virtue in snapping
a record of this vacancy. Alone. As proof
of our hiding-place, a green stage for

whatever did or didn't happen on
five days. Look at it either way. I'll take
another route back to the car. Scarlet
Fly Agaric by a birch-tree, pastures
and church-towers to the east. The rain
held off. Dark clouds just skimmed the hilltops
and the wind blew cold. Beyond the gusts
I could not catch your voice. Each faltering
step seemed now so unfamiliar.
I groped for the compass, wondering
who'd lugged the blame along. Back home once more
I found a single harebell pressed between
two summer pages of my battered Schoolboy's
Diary – dry, skeletal, possessing one less
dimension than reality. So like the past.

Craft

So bring the invisible full into play
– BROWNING

Retrospective

for Peter Thursby

A portrait you did of yourself
at eighteen hangs in one corner –
confident, flaunting a new blue
chin, a touch wary, pugnacious
even, schooled in fierce encounters
at water-polo – already
so skilful, features in vibrant
perspective, background suggested
casually.
             The room holds your bright
harvest – a trio of figures
in front of flames, sculptures half black
half silver, whirl of a farmyard
cock with scimitars for feathers,
bronze struts dazzled by spray, cobalt
sun crowning ghost-hint of a tree.

You couldn't see them all those years
ago. The fact they're there now proves
that adolescent knew just what
had to be done. He possessed iron
loyalty to his vision, love
of textures, hunger for colour,
calm-fevered need to conquer fresh
realms of design. The victory
in embryo is his while this
fulfilment nowadays is yours
for all we're celebrating here
has been foreshadowed in those eyes.

Dorset County Museum
Dorchester, January, 2008

Two Walls

for Cory once again

1   Spread of flood. Sea-birds in flight above
and to the side. Three of them –
white, blue, flurry of wings.
Unmoving. Fixed in brightness. Each
an archaeopteryx flung live
against an Arctic June.

2   Shore line now. Foam-margin
drawn in sand. And on a shelf stand blocks –
small monoliths, relic
of an abandoned breakwater.

3   Dissolving figures along a path
in some coloured forest aching to discern
a phantom message written
by autumn clouds.

4   Her ochre back, the erotic two-
dimensioned self abstracted.
Once, yes, the skin was real but now,
transmuted, one key-moment caught.
Arête between depiction and discovery.
Form. Torso unearthed among rubble.
Hot field in Greece
near a shore again
under no flying birds.

The Poetry of Ideas

Triple colours
figuring in
Duke Ellington's
jazz suite were black,
brown and beige. This
dismal day in
high summer, green,
brown and grey formed
the sole palette
available
in the dark woods –
foliage, grass,
bracken, berries
unripened
    then
tree-trunks, packed earth
of the trodden
path, last autumn's
leaves shrivelled
     then
above the skeined
tracery clouds
unrelenting
with their sullen
prospect of rain.

I veered to pee
behind a dank
screen of holly
near the fringes
of the wood where
fields of July
wheat rimmed by hedge-
rows continued

the first colour;
new five-barred gates,
withered stalks, piles
of pale soil lent
khaki; still ponds
mirrored pewter
smudges along
the threatened sky
while smoke drifted
from one unseen
cottage which could
boast yellow walls
not to say a
gaudy muster
of hollyhocks
to interrupt
the going scheme.

And so relieved
finding now how
landscapes beyond
also honoured
the patched season
I turned away
with one more aim
in mind this time
at least to use
no sophistry
trying to match
foxed secrecy
inside the wood.

Henry Scott Tuke: *Noonday Heat, 1903*

Two youths. One, stripped to the waist,
white trousers to his navel,
sprawls on the sand looking up
at another who, naked,
kneeling sideways propped on one
arm, head and shoulders in grey
shadow, gazes down meeting
his eyes with what can only
be desire. A green cove glints
beyond. Dark cliffs shutting off
any hint of sea or sky
allow no alternative.

Falmouth Art Gallery, June, 2008

On the Shore

for Kevin Bailey

He breathed dark salt air
standing on cold sand and shells
    to assess the west:
    waves flecked with spindrift
long silhouette of black rock
    sky one haze of stars.
    Island of exile
for a wily ex-emperor
    and a priest who left
    footprints in the snow.
They'd sentenced him to death but
    the sword-blade shattered
    touching his bared nape.
In Kugahara we'd hear
    the great bell booming
    from the hill-temple
Nichiren founded. Later,
    a banished playwright
    walking by the sea
recalled white petals falling
    on an outspread fan.
    Gold got discovered
after silver-lodes had been
    mined for centuries –
    a deft example
of business know-how coming
    late to a jackpot.
    Bashô saw time streaked
with bleak twists of history.
    Transient mankind seemed
    less fine than the sheen

as that immobile river
　　　of paradise flowed
　　　across the night sky
unperturbed by loneliness
　　　or greed. He found swirls
　　　of destiny in
the wet tumult of the strait
　　　and retired early.
　　　Whores next door kept him
awake as they mourned their life
　　　having to pretend
　　　their love for client
after client. Next morning
　　　outside the inn they
　　　asked to go with him.
It could not be. They wept. He
　　　left them with pity.

Reality at More than One Remove

Red sand
And the harbour's been turned into
tokens of green gravel
Hills in the distance shift pink past ochre
close to a sky of scurried leaves
One wall has faded to a yard
where a dog is involved in scratching itself
Tulips push through the roof-tiles
Clumps of blue trees may be noon clouds
or else the far sea
waveless   untenanted by liners

Objects get labelled *green* and *ochre*
but the poem's colourblind
with the painter's
patent success transmuted
into greyish paper   ink-smeared words
And what was meant by it
        (the teasing vibrancy
        that snare of non-perspective)
I've lost but he
(or was it she?)
still holds

I find in cold retrospect that I'm
unable to remember in what gallery
or even on which occasion
how far back
I stood before the canvas
gleefully baffled

About the Statues

I   One wouldn't want them golden-
     haired or tricked out with flesh-tints
     to delude wistful glances.
     They don't own reality
     weren't even meant to nor prove
     a substitute for desire
     simply offering just out
     of reach the consolation
     of a curve, the perfect tense
     in stone plucked free from time. No
     more. And life-size isn't that
     important. No unwieldy
     conception of a titan
     nor a ten-inch figurine
     on his escritoire for some
     dilettante to finger
     the right hand busy scrawling
     recollections of the Grand
     Tour – dalliance, temperatures,
     meals, mileages and so forth.

II   Creamiest marble. About
     five and a half feet tall.
     No leaves were rustling on the plaza.
     A harsh midday
     stamped a distorted square inside the door.

     In Cretan shadows a breeze has lifted your cloak
     baring the form from navel downwards.
     One slim leg's advanced to pretend you're heading
     too eagerly for somewhere. Your bland gaze
     under the faintest scratch of a frown
     may be aware that rain could drift quite soon.

So you stand
shouldering that absent wind
away from this museum
on the other side of time.
One palm's held flat shading your eyes
to make out whatever
the sculptor imagined you could see –
parched boulders, a grey olive-tree,
some goats, a glimpse of white peaks,
the downslope glint of a gulf.

III   The sunstruck gateway to a park.
Pallor swivelling ripples up from a river
on to scabby plane-trunks, underside
of a bridge-arch.
                        Winged ankles,
spread figleaf like a protecting hand,
stripped torso, helmet also tipped with wings.

Further on, below a forested hill,
the sacred spring
concealed by an ornamental pool
breaks the surface
as a scimitar of disruption
cold froth on green
watched over by a shepherd-boy
who's forgotten his flock never grazed here
and doesn't suspect the presence
of the imminent hovering eagle.

IV   To study them in the open
suffering skies of one colour or another
snow-garlanded perhaps or stroked by moonlight
is no more appropriate
than in some hall where footsteps click and echo.
            'The consolation of a curve.'
Sensuous. Unsensual. The pledge
beauty can exist in space
resisting time. About delight
as much as ruefulness.

          To pace away from where you are
and go to where you never can
be then or now. And so move back
back through the forbidden gate you
didn't notice when you entered
to face the fact reality
       so often lets us down.

Xarnia–Nîmes–Avignon

Beyond the Rim

Le temps s'en va, le temps s'en va, ma dame,
Las! le temps non, mais nous, nous en allons

– RONSARD

Time fades away, my lady, fades away,
Alas, not time, no, we're the ones who fade

In Memory of David Henderson

You were unwell when I arrived.
Courteous as ever, you contrived
To welcome me and show off books
You'd bought once for a song. Though looks
Deceive, I feared for you – so frail,
So wasted. Breath and heart will fail
The best of us. Did you admit
That vodka downed, tobacco lit,
Reduced you captive to that room?
Man's the constructor of his doom
And maps his future blindly. How
To help was not the issue now.
You never asked for sympathy
And kept things in proportion by
A sense of the ridiculous.
The world got put to rights by us
With laughter and quotation. I
Admired your courage and your dry
Dismissal of pretentiousness.

You died within the week. Unless
We go on citing those we knew
The memories they loved die too.
I want to register each phrase
That kept your past alive – those days
With stingy uncles at the zoo,
Those bouts with Greek, that voyage to
The Faroes, boxing-matches won,
Odd dramas acted in for fun.

Your legacy is more than these –
For students (who are hard to please)
Have you to thank for insights shared,
Enthusiasm, theories dared,

Unorthodox approaches that
Made all received ideas fall flat.
Teachers live on in those they taught
(For better or for worse). You thought
Your students should *enjoy* a text –
Sheer pleasure first, assessment next.
Knowing your faults (which they forgave)
They stand indebted at your grave.

A Letter

in memory of Ric Caddel

Dear Ric,
            Last summer in Japan, your six
responses to a coast you loved conveyed
the salt tang of the North Sea flickering
with puffins to a land you'd seen the year
before, whose clean trains, temples, fabulous
department-stores filled you with awe. I hope
your ears burned at the praise those crisp lines raised
from foreign readers.
                Poet, rambler, sage,
most generous of publishers, your speech
was spiced with laughter – your quicksilver mind
lit up the silly side of things although
you never once sold short a relish for
out-of-the-way glints of pure scholarship –
Cretaceous flora, contrapuntal song,
Chinese philosophy, Welsh legends.
                     So
you were against syllabics! I can't take
one of your heroes, that New Jersey quack!
Cherished companions, heaven knows, are meant
to differ else concourse would sound so bland.

I have a photograph I treasure: you
in black-and-white and thoughtful as you pay
benign attention to some poet's voice,
a pint half empty in your hand.
                I wish
I could replenish one for you to-day
and listen to you speak so wisely, shed
doubt over my intolerance and set
us treading on a more exacting path.

You knew great grief and have passed on to us
the need to mourn a jagged gap in life
you've left. Maybe, who knows, beyond that blank
no-one can vouch for we can walk again
to Wistman's Wood and talk as spirits talk.

If now all those who knew your work are sad,
you're missed far more by those who knew you, those
who had that privilege.
Love,
Harry Guest

Rock-Cut Tomb

I.M. Peter Redgrove

Why go to the high island
infertile even hostile
where skuas swoop to distract you
and a hare lollops over the heather

For the grey block
the gaping hole
the stone plug left by the entrance

I see

Though your concerns were rarely mine
my loves not parallel to yours
I find your way of logging toad-track moon-phase wasp-flight
admirable
like your eccentric mirror to the womb

The road we came by runs far across the valley
This ledge where bones lay spreads flat and scoured
Crouching on the sandstone floor
a visitor peers out at clumps of bog-cotton
hears the sea

The skulls here saw only blackness

We can push the door open
It's made of sunlight

Dwarfie Stane
Hoy
June 2003

3 p.m. September 18th 2004

for Penelope
in memory of Peter Redgrove

Ashes to water
tideflow will coax
cradled by moonchange
placated by wind

Offered from shore
now one with creation
all he encountered
weighed wrote of and knew

Spirit not wholly
absent still present
in those salt whispers
acknowledged on sand

May memory guard him
each reader revive him
all rainbows mourn one
who loved what he saw

Thom Gunn 1929–2004

We last met outside Charing Cross by chance,
your cowboy boots contrasting with my own
scuffed suèdes. Cambridge post-war seemed far away
(Dadie v. Leavis, *Chequer*, tea with Karl)
though oddly less so later when the oracles
deigned to reveal their flip-side.
                                    With dismay
I came to learn how, on that boring Coast,
you had succumbed to drug-abuse – for that
diminishes a man and you had stood
(in lofty footwear) for the classic values
of rigour, dedication to the task,
a legacy adapted early on
from Wyatt's masculine diplomacy.
You wrote of sex too as if Attic warriors
just tussled playfully – but never shirked
gauging the chill of anonymity till fear
brought out imaginary beads of venom
in the small hours.
                    You stay in memory
as generous and unaffected, your talk
glinting with merriment, your work
inventive, knotty, scrupulous.
                                It's hard
to feel you're gone like Hughes, like Redgrove. Since
the Fifties you were always *there*. At least
each poem wryly wrought will carry on
flexing its sinews for us when we scan.
I know you know we know how good they are.

Taking Us On

I.M. Trevor Goodman

For *Private View* you wanted '*painter*' added
to the dedication, lifting you away
from anonymities like '*friend*' or '*teacher*' since
the first would trap you in an arcane rôle –
unshared, unshareable – and the second just
sprinkle chalk-dust on a gown you never wore.
Your influence on pupils stretched beyond
the artist's craft with cure and music. One
became a surgeon and another, sadly
preceding you in death, built harpsichords.
Still, his self-portrait as a moody youth
(pale face the sole relief from indigo)
hangs on my study-wall just opposite
your radiant zigzag of North Cornwall where
hedgerows criss-cross in hints like that décor
you dreamed up slinging ropes to cast green shadows
on Fry's miracle-play about Saint Cuthman.

Spring in St. Ives, your studio accepting
the grey blaze of the sea. We put *Les Francs-Juges*
(controlled of course by Beecham) on the pick-up.
Tea with Linden Travers. I was so thrilled
and certainly tongue-tied (you never were)
to meet the siren from that Hitchcock film.
We trekked to Zennor once along the coast
(a change from pillion on your motorbike)
and drank I'm sure far too much beer there with
Graham and Lanyon who'd mislaid their wives.
I'd just been given *The Night-Fishing* so
felt bolder but had not yet seen those tall
vertiginous accounts of shore and moorland
seen from the sky. Much missed, the three of you

up there somewhere beyond the clouds must be
expounding pure abstraction to the angels.

You taught me Gowing's views on Rembrandt, why
Velázquez stayed your perfect painter, where
Watteau's brush (never cleaned) left pigments, how
Turner wrapped mists of gold round distance, who
Picasso thought he might turn into, what
Paul Nash meant with his megaliths and when
Cézanne's fruits rotted nobly in their bowl.
You never signed your paintings. Tapping one,
your puritan headmaster said 'The sin
of pride'. Unlike him you spread joy in life,
told us to smile not mope, try this and that,
communicate with praise not carp or sneer.

You could out-argue any philistine,
flew high the flag of culture and delight,
kept serious about your art and claimed
the human body offers all the shapes
an artist needs. 'And colour too sometimes'
you'd add. One freezing morning at your art-school
the naked model had to strike a pose
between iron stove and winter window so
half of her turned bright blue, half mottled scarlet.

So near my heart still, you are still around
in paint, inaccuracies, photos, books,
records and laughter often. It was hard
those last months on the 'phone hearing you say
you wished to fall asleep and not wake up.
Kind Time has granted that at last, dear Trev,
bequeathing me a grief that's here to stay.

Envoi

Lying in both senses about the past
like sarsens strewn on grass we never saw
but boasted of. Or a scarf flung over
a chair somewhere recalled although by now
dyed the wrong colour in the mind. Still pool
reed-fringed still proved by memory but placed
in a different county even photo'd there.
Untruths need not be conscious. You repeat
what you believe occurred and put it down
glowing, intact. Experts not wise to what
they're up to can perform this beautifully.
One friend unnamed smiles near a cliff where there
were fewer fossils or was that the reason.
Disjointed references perplex the wary.
Façades far less symmetric have been warped
by no disloyalty unlike that heavy
tape-recorder spooling whose poems to
oblivion. The instance of a Chinese
tea-cup lifted to ghost-lips as the clock
chimes five with noon at the window. A pair
of rainbows tailed the Buick all day long
but who was driving. Fading tesserae
fake things which never happened like the god
with a blurred sword not clutching the familiar
bunch of grapes. Which is why there's no question-
mark on the keyboard. No-one can explain
eyelids now hiding those blue irises
remembered in the family portrait
which used to hang on the lower landing.
The dead haul with them certain truisms
misheard with amazement or dismay. Values
once owned must start to tantalise. It may
well be this is what sorrow's all about.

For Whose Eyes Only

Aus der Jugendzeit, aus der Jugendzeit
Klingt ein Lied mir immerdar;
O wie liegt so weit, o wie liegt so weit,
Was mein einst war!

— FRIEDRICH RÜCKERT

Out of youth's bright day, out of youth's bright day,
Sounds for ever one refrain:
Now so far away, now so far away,
What once was gain!

For Whose Eyes Only

Gratitude

Your beauty like a thunderbolt attacked
the way I looked at things. The world around
burned in new colours and I didn't dare
crash through the wonder to get near you. So
it took some weeks of sleeplessness before
I plucked up the effrontery to – What?
Well . . . woo you down from that gold shelf among
the clouds although I must confess I'd put
you there myself. This can't be a lament.
We came unclasped without a wan pretence
of plangency – I doubt we even knew
that call it our affair had fizzled out.
Coming of age we picked careers and failed
to keep in touch. And I suspect the glow
I treasure faded swiftly for you (if
indeed you ever felt one) but this builds
no barrier when I'm drawn to reminisce.
I've written so dishonestly in prose –
that novel I suspect you didn't read –
about these matters which now matter less
than ever or maybe I mean much more.
It's hard to hold the past in place using
a rope of fog. All my activities
were limited by love or so I thought
back then. How could I mind when the rewards
though paltry seemed immense? You taught me how
to kiss and in your bed infrequently
(aware the outer door stayed bolted) I
found safety in our sameness whereas you
regarded what we did as second-best.
I see that now but tried to hide it then
drumming up fantasies to waste dry days

and keep me callow. Did you know I watched
you with amazement all the time? Dawns seemed
to happen only when we met. You lent
me all I dreamed you owned until I crossed
the Rubicon (or Cam) to manhood. On
that nearer shore we'd offered secrecy.
Not for one moment were we haunted by
that idiotic law – not like my smuggling
Ulysses or the works of Genet back
from Paris in a muddle of used socks.
Our contraband could not be labelled. Through
the window (mine – not yours which faced, you may
recall, the Arctic) sunlight drifting on
our nakedness encouraged attitudes
untampered with not omens for July.
Friends, studies, commonsense all prowled outside
the hedges cultivated by – may I
just use the word? – our passion. We'd become
the unsuspected duo far away
from masks, pale alibis and the barbed-wire
lasso of scorn. Once we'd got rid of time
we tried to opt out in the name of love
evading truth and finding nothing else.

Pact

We watched a flaring thunderstorm
and stood together with the pane
one blaze of sheer gold to perform
a rite so equalled each could gain
control of conquest yet submit
to subjugation: paradox
unlike some less baroquely lit
in other rooms where faulty clocks
still rang the change on words like us.

You'd always alter though in those
lost days while I – despite the fuss
of moving – kept, so I suppose,
the same self, making good each debt.
By chance a photo published by
the local paper (I forget
its name now) captured that same sky
at three a.m. (the hour when we
were swapping rôles) scrawled by five lines
of lightning setting every tree
alight with white – cloudy designs
turned on and off as the display
waged by electric titans stayed
nonstop. I can't recall the way
the end came (who first?). That air-raid
though – rowdy, mimicking the War
by that time over – carried on
long after I'd detected your
last gasp (you mine). The truce once won
made up for any loss incurred.
To-morrow on its way, we kissed,
reluctant to risk any word,
picked scattered clothes up and got dressed.

Fidelity

Too long ago now. Hard to think
how much I took for granted then.
So quickly over. Plus a blank
before and after. Yet each dawn
that week in Paris stays as clear.
Light probing the uncurtained room.
A gauloise shared on waking. Shower
together kissing under warm
pretence of rainfall. Shamelessly

we'd put off trudging down to face
sly glances when we left the key
and towel each other in the glass
which hadn't questioned what we did
or were. The days spread welcome for
unfettered plans. The other bed
to rumple. Lunch late. Art show or
a film. I was still unattached
and young. You younger. You could say
each had seduced the other, reached
a private contract with the way
things seemed to be. Walking beside
that Sussex river in the dark
began it all. And if we lied
reluctance hasn't left a mark
on either. Did I mind the fact
you loved another? I required
co-operation in the act.
No more. You'd anyway grow tired
of my attentions. Letters sent.
Phone-calls bled dry since someone might
be eavesdropping. A frown which meant
you'd sooner be alone. The night
once over though merely to see
the blue smoke eddying from your mouth.
Such half-hearted complicity
felt for a time enough. We'd both
agreed to shrug off any claim.
Your farewell would with hindsight prove
my rescue once I'd learned to aim
no longer to the left of love.

'Any Time'

An echo from your
soft mouth. Only three
syllables heard in
that dark café of
staccato memory.
On the table two
half-empty tumblers
of Kirin beer. Blue
fish indolently
darted in their lit
glass gaol to your left.
Our glances met to
flinch aside again.
Past desultory talk
I felt half-certain
alluring by-ways
waited while we drew
alternate puffs from
my last cigarette –
a Hi-Lite, rather
acrid. In the class
that evening (you may
remember) I'd taught
Othello. Prelude
for stripped deceits in
that ryokan across
the alleyway. When
the bland landlady
spread a red futon
on the tatami
she'd always say 'Go
yukkuri' (meaning
'Take your time'). After
such switch in language
acting our rôle as

robbers was a cinch.
Learning to run off
with hours we knew weren't
ours to lift or own.
Alibis found for
missing afternoons.
Scribbled lies in lieu
of whereabouts on
phantom schedules. As
camouflage. For what?
You never told me.
Even now so much
stays wrapped in wonder.
That first occasion
though – wary, weighing
each flicker of a
reaction – we fenced
with phrases, our legs
just touching, till my
dry tongue managed 'I'd
like to. When?' And then
you said

The Crystal Cabinet

The Madonna with the green woodpecker,
The Madonna of the fig-tree,
The Madonna beside the yellow dam,
Turn their kind faces from us
And our projects under construction,
Look only in one direction,
Fix their gaze on our completed work

– W. H. Auden

Divans

for A. L. Hendriks

Lounging on one
in Persia or
leafing through one
to please or bore . . .
Yes, *couch* or *set*
of poems – yet
it seems you call
that *Customs-Hall*
we scurry though
in ones or twos
with fags and booze
a *divan* too.

Poets can't claim
immunity.
The rule's the same –
if duty-free
that minimum
demand's still fair:
'Have you got some-
thing to declare?'

Episodes

April 15th
18:30

Evening. The bougainvillaea
almost colourless. White Rolls
parked, right-hand drive.
Scarlet clouds staining windscreen.
Map of the city on back seat;
travelling-rug; binoculars.

April 15th
11:45

Slim windows ajar
on to balcony. No wind.
Body half in bright sunlight;
blood spilt near marquetry table.
Two wineglasses. Lipsticked cigarette
in marble ashtray.

April 14th
19:00

Talk, laughter, in the high room.
Lawns darkening as lights
prick on in the murky harbour.
Frogged uniforms, champagne,
orders worn. Honey-skinned youth
in evening dress smiles once more
catching his eye across the gathering.

April 16th
08:00

Wet newspaper spread on chair-back
to dry. UNEXPLAINED DEATH
OF PROMINENT DIPLOMAT. The bracts
glisten beyond window in rain.
Smell of coffee, hot bread. White top
glimpsed across road. One
mackintoshed policeman
peering down from opposite balcony.

April 14th
11:45

Empty chair at café table.
Square a brilliant yellow.

Awning thwacked by the breeze.
Tall glass before her. Dark lenses,
large hat. Impatiently
glances at her watch.

April 15th
07:00 Street empty. Hint of dew
on the groomed gardens.
Briefcase on passenger seat,
stole draped across, also a map
carefully folded.

April 14th
11:45 Youth plunges shivering
into wind-flung spray. The rocks
seem deserted. He races him
along beach to get warm
before picnicking in the Rolls.

April 14th
20:15 Light from the open mahogany
door falls on the curve of gravel.
Slender woman, orchid in her hand,
waits on the flight of steps,
stole gathered around her.
Thin wind under the rising moon
makes the wistaria tremble.
The Rolls pulls up.

April 14th
23:30 Room silent except for their sleep.
Moonlight through drawn curtains colours
gracefully their casual limbs.

April 15th
12:00 Male figure unhurrying
crosses street. Grey Fiat
moves out from behind parked van.
Parallel with the Rolls,
stops. Noon siren from factory.
Man now between cars.

Slam of two doors. The Fiat
descends the boulevard,
woman driving. No-one now
on road or sidewalk.

April 15th
23:30

No moon. Only the street-lamps
and winking lights on the police-cars.
First prickle of rain.

Before Reflection

If thought is thunder
    All ideas are ice
Glaciers will sunder
    While white peaks entice

When peril beckons
    Intrepid desire
A wise wife reckons
    On curbing the fire

Caution prevailing
    Once ways have been weighed
Never plain sailing
    Few swords lack a blade

Better for ever
    Though missing one day
Nothing should sever
    A craft from its bay

Arctic clouds heaping
    Their threat in the air
Mean we'll be keeping
    Leg-irons on despair

With candle-fed faith
    Anxieties lure
If hope's just a wraith
    Attempt may be cure

Stammered auguries
    Confuse now with then
And trust in decrees
    From guts of a hen

Dimmed lodestars forsake
    Those not in the know
Philosophies take
    The off-chance in tow

Yesterday's sorrow
    Calls out in advance
And each to-morrow
    Has led us a dance

Greased court-cards foretell
    What won't come to pass
No bright pimpernel
    But bloodspot on grass

Three Word-Sonnets

Cold
day.

Stay.

Hold
fast
this
kiss.

Last
chance.

Merc
friends.

Dance
ends
here.

Still
light . . .

Will
night
feel
you
steal
through?

Fate's
lot
states
not.

When
then?

Must
my
lust
die?

Our
red
hour
fled.

You
are
too
far.

I
sigh.

Florum Imagines

I   *Violets*

Their colour draws darkness
from the wrong side of the soil

They give the daytime back as night –
sparks from those grief-lamps
hung on ceilings of the silent kingdom
in lieu of stars

They hint at an afterworld
shining with mourning –
at moments draped in shadow
                         in sorrow
and summers muffled
beyond the reach of light
                      of normal light

II   *Camellias*

From this window
the cold pink
of their discs
holds less glow
than the leaves
surrounding them
so forms spaces
able to banish
all colour save
their own seeming
not to stir
in the heavy
spring rain falling

III   *Dandelion*

Yellow, it follows
the sun to the west

In autumn grey stars
fixed to thin needles
form a sphere of seeds
counting the hour
when children make moments
drift over grass

A pitted bald head
is all that gets left
once time has been told

IV   *White Rose*

One bloom, swaying,
reveals the gold dust at its heart

The breeze dies and petals
stay glued to the air

Its scent
entrances the stillness –
its pallor a mere
absence of tone, a blank
defying the eye,
betraying no interest
in gaining an advocate

Leaves lining the stem
look cold and drab –
tiny red thorns though
offer a warning

v   *Speedwells*

A healing farness
urges our gaze
beyond all the milestones
set by the spring
displaying proof of a spaciousness
hard to credit
beneath the autocracy of low noons

Now, unconfined,
February's tyrant fled,
we walk still barely able to trust
a newfound species of freedom

Insignificant holes
punched in the green laneside
are letting in the first
immensity of light

Arethusa

She came to the bank of a river
so clear it seemed not to be flowing.
Some silver leaves dark in the water –
deep, wavering every so often –
gave proof they were just a reflection.

    She slid naked into the stream.
    The god of the place slipped between
    her breasts, past her thighs, till she fled
    downriver, crawled on to dry land
    and hid in a shadow of mist.

    He traced her from drips on the grass.
She entered again his embraces.
    Together they stole from the sun.
Slim nymph and cool river coiled gliding
    as one along underground caves.

Away from the fields of her childhood
    through echoing chambers of death
they swirled on absorbed in each other.
    Dawn found them a gate in the rock.
This led to a lake. Not a ripple
    disturbed the tranquillity. Now
pursuer, pursued had no meaning.
    The aim and the target changed rôles.

Riddle

Thing crouched behind word
springs into language

(Hidden by riddle
thing sidesteps with sly
winks at the reader)

No fragrance yet the fold
translated to pallor
of sulphur on gold draws
back summer dusks freighted
with memory – head bent
in anticipation
of pleasure – albeit
these overlapping flakes
(ivory shadow-furred)
offer the expectant
touch no texture except
a bland slipperiness –
however, seen edge-on,
this instant taken out
of time rules an almost
undetectable white
line in the lighted room
and if turned in the hand
will reveal when reversed
the disquieting fact
there's nothing behind it

Thing riddle-concealed
slinks off with a shy
glance at the puzzler

(Thing spotlit by word
stammers a meaning)

ANSWER: A BLACK AND WHITE PHOTOGRAPH

A Song for Autumn

Sad autumn tones
While violins
    Languish
Hurt my weary
Heart with dreary
    Anguish

Gone pale and wan
And breathless when
    Hours chime
I cry when I
Remember by-
    gone time

An ill breeze grieves
Me as I stray
    Away
Like shrivelled leaves
Driven this way
    That way

Verlaine, Chanson d'automne

When Orpheus Sings

A tree arose – conquest of pure transcendence –
(when Orpheus sings tall trees spring in the ear)
and all fell silent, yet, within that silence,
knew newness, hearing signs and change draw near.

Creatures emerged from lair and nest inside
the loosened wood compelled by secrecy –
and it was not that they were terrified
or sly that they obeyed so easily.

They had been listening. To growl, cry, roar
seemed paltry to them now. And while they saw
no hut prepared though they'd come here to hear –

no refuge formed from darkest longing set
with trembling door-posts – he did not forget
to build a temple for them in each ear.

Rilke, Die Sonette an Orpheus, Erster Teil, 1

Under the Constellation of Hercules

Somewhere
no bigger
than the circle
a hawk might trace
on the sky at dusk.

A wall rough-
hewn burnt
by reddish moss.
A distant bell conveying
the smoke of olive-trees
over shimmering water.
Fire
fed by straw
and damp foliage
filtered by voices
you don't recognize.

Submitting to the night
to its icy harness
Hercules draws the chain-
harrow of stars
up the northern sky.

Peter Huchel, Unterm Sternbild des Hercules

Leafing through Old Manuscripts

Your own time is here
translated into lucid symbols.
Hopes didn't get fulfilled,
what you loved turned away from you.

'Promise me you'll . . .'
Memory points to
evening, rainfall, delicate hair.

Leafing through old manuscripts
on a Sunday afternoon
– when it's gone quiet and clouds darken the light –
I want to appease the shadows
which have a grip on my throat.

Walter Neumann, In alten Manuskripten lesend

What is Certain

Morning lying
over the mountains.

Warmth of water
rinsing night from your hands.

The friendly
rustle of a newspaper.

The even tread
of my neighbour
on the stairs.

The click as my past
gets locked away.

Going out into a day
which places wind on my face.

Taking back words
that haven't been spoken.

The subjunctive of the opposite.

Hans Dieter Schmidt, Was sicher ist

Johannes Bobrowski's House

It's such a relief
to know about your redcurrant-bushes
and, oh yes, in spring I forgot to mention
the garden-fence could do with a lick of paint

But then if autumn isn't over
the maple-leaves won't come to any harm
in the gentle hands of your children

Of course
there's their mother going through the house
and there's the return home each day
and the tall doorway
to come in through from the dark

I'd think of the old sister too
but she hurries on her stick from grief to grief

It's good
to wait for dawn
anyway: we're getting ready

Rolf Haufs, Bei Johannes Bobrowski

Return to Campoformido

to my father, the aviator

Going back to Campoformido
it's as though that photo –
the one of you in your flying-suit
standing among others in your squadron
your face disclosed to the future –
had never actually been taken

Going back to Campoformido
it's as though you stepped suddenly
out of the family album
one moonless evening
to recover a glimmer of youth
a brilliance of wings
submitting neither to the wind
nor to the tendency of time to fade

Going back to Campoformido
it's as though with the wave of a wand
you turned twenty again and wearing
the smile of a conspirator asked me
to detach our two shadows from the ground
and get ready for take-off together
without our parachutes

Daniele Serafini, Ritorno a Campoformido

Inventory: Homage to Jacques Prévert

Two Elizabethan miniatures, one Jacobean tragedy, one Caroline succession, one Regency terrace, one Victorian horror, one Edwardian afternoon.

Five finger exercises, four quartets, three blind mice, two lilywhite boys, one pair of hands.

One gaudy night.

Twelve honest men and true, three months without the option, twenty-two yards.

One chain.

First light, second sight, third time lucky, fourth dimension, fifth avenue, sixth sense, seventh seal, eighth army, forty-ninth parallel, eleventh hour, twelfth man.

Four Bills, eight Hals, one Steve, eight Teds, two Jims, two Charlies.

Two Lizzies, two Maries, one Anne.

Three guineas. Two gentlemen of Verona. One tale of two cities. Seven samurai. Three men in a boat. One way pendulum.

To say nothing of the dog.

Two years before the mast. Four feathers. Nine pins. Three card tricks. Six of the best. Four corners of the earth. One wonder. Two Tudors. Four forgers. Ten tenders. One book of revelation. Half a dozen of the other.

Six of one.

Nine tailors. Ten green bottles. Thirty-nine articles. Six proud walkers. Seven maids (with seven mops). One partridge (in a pear-tree).

No fear. No name. No bed for Bacon. No room at the inn. No time to argue.

Two for the price of one.

Three legged races. Three cornered hats. Three bags full.

Forty winks. Four posters. Forty pianos. Fourscore years and ten. One rod, pole or perch. Sixteen ounces.

One pound. Fourteen pounds.

One stone.

Six Haiku

Brilliant dew on the flower
vanishing soon after sunrise.
When will the petals fall?

– *Sôgi* (1421–1502)

June rainfall constant
       just on one night
          moongleam through pines

– *Ryôta* (1718–87)

Someone's stuck his finger
through the paper window.
        Look!
        Stars!

– *Issa* (1762–1826)

Alone again after
the firework display.
Starless darkness

– *Shiki* (1867–1902)

Unmoving river
a summer sunset
      boat tethered
      rusty iron
      glints in the water

– *Yamaguchi Seishi* (1901–94)

Midwinter footprints
leading to dusk or sunrise
crisscross on the snow

These Days

Il faut être absolument moderne
– RIMBAUD

It's essential to keep up to date

The Truth of Blue

We know by now that sapphires can be red
(garnets grass-green too – rubies indigo)
just mimicking another gem instead
of flaunting what they really are, that glow

flicked by a wave at sunrise or the sky
when no rain's threatened. So I'll celebrate
to-day our jewel's old identity
as blue as Mary's robe, a paperweight

of dark Czech glass, the level flash along
a stream each time a kingfisher flies by,
delphiniums near grey walls, glints which belong
to a baby's marvelling eyes, to purity

and wonder, to immensity and calm . . .
Sea . . . Twilight . . .
                        Forty-five years.
                                        A past tense
with so much.
                Wear this necklace as a charm
to ward off shifts in colour, make all dense

blocks of obsidian keep black, snows hold
their whiteness, pimpernels quite stubbornly
stay scarlet and the future's store of gold
shine uninfected with duplicity.

December 28th, 2008

In the Tourist Office

Assure the autumn you intend no harm
to darkness circling underneath the alders.
A stag will pace past thinning foliage,
each river overflow its banks, the moor
choose tans and purples to replace the green.

What happens when the whinchat leaves affects
the hiker and hotelier no less.
Should week-ends drizzle, scarlet coastlines still
invigorate the gaze. Though granite-cold
the churches (some unlocked) hold mysteries
worth prising from their shadows.

                              When the snow
falls on the tor recall how primroses
will star the lanes again and five-year-olds
build sand-defences which can't stem the tide.

Each phase is welcome and not meant to last.
The seasons here shuffle the light with skill.

Seas

for Owen Davis on his 70th birthday

Standing on cliffs of an island which isn't really an island
you'll see a disused quarry below you blurred with spindrift.
Half-carved blocks of marble which isn't really marble wait
for the ghost-ships which will never come back to return.
Near here we once read our poems to people by candlelight.
The lawns I remember sloped to sand, and far away over
the dark channel a pattern of tiny windows glimmered
on the Isle of Wight which *is* surrounded by water.
Liners in wartime took us off to different foreign
locations. Enemy dive-bombers criss-crossed each Pacific
stretch of sky between islands and submarines quartered
the Gulf Stream under convoys. There may not have been
a future for either of us but here we both are, having
slipped past yet another climacteric. Seas you see
stay enigmatic in their colouring, sometimes as gold
as credence, at other moments grey like a fond deception
or a blue never to be recorded, a green you can't define
(or wish to), silver dwindling from west to east as cat's-paws
tease mat surfaces. And tides are 'always begun again'
as the poet wrote in a churchyard (not you nor I). Unsquared
rafts of purple under their clouds urge you to voyage outside
the quirks of time, old age, forgetfulness, the absence
of those we loved – but seas are cleansing places despite
the wrong activities of man and on a birthday
stand for discovery not stasis. The salter tang of truth.

The Cranes Are Silent

Structures half-done or quarter-done
jut here and there along the skyline

Spaces cleared for office-blocks
flattened areas of volcanic rubble
left empty
        Down tools!
               The crash
re-echoed round the world. The cause?
Incompetence of course but also greed
the Deadly Sin which claws from others
what it wants

And so no workers needed for the moment
Homes forfeited
Future uneasy

However

Those properties   and sites   and mechanisms
(now in abeyance)
have all been bought up by the banks

In offices thumbs are twirling patiently

Sooner or later
the undeserved millions will treble again

Meanwhile
along the skyline
the cranes are silent

Reykjavík, August, 2009

Sleepless by You

Where are you now? Watching the dark I hear
you breathe and feel your warmth but you're far off
tangled in dream. Your footfalls make no sound
as you keep going past façades which have
nothing behind them. I shall never know
what murmurings you detect, what pointless shifts
of time and place you take for granted in
that realm where things though as they never were
appear familiar.
                          You sigh at times
betraying neither pleasure nor alarm –
certainly not surprise when those long dead
beckon from shadows and two black cats we
still miss whisk past. Vicinity, it seems,
convinces. Somehow the remote lacks all
importance. Anyway what's close is bound
to alter or get casually replaced
once unexpectedness became the norm.

Is no provision made for stasis? Do
you roam unclear of whereabouts (the way,
darling, you do so readily in life)
walking unwilled – a magnet being drawn
to destinations always out of reach?
I'd like to pace beside you but perhaps
my presence is unwelcome in a dream.
Sleep may imply escape from self but still
more crucially from other people too.
To be alone. Unworried by events
that tease and quiver. And to hear advice
you can not only disagree with but
ignore. Live by yourself without your self.
Eyes closed yet peering at discovery.

AND IF A CROSSROAD DISAPPEARS OR ROCKS
ROLL NOISELESSLY TOWARDS YOU AS A HAND
THRUSTS YOU INTO THEIR PATH OR THERE'S A PLEA
FOR RESCUE THOUGH YOU CAN'T SEE WHERE IT'S COME
FROM OR THE WATER'S RISING IN SOME ROOM
LACKING A DOOR OR INEXPLICABLY
YOU'RE STANDING IN SOME POLAR WASTE WITH NO
HORIZON YET THE SKY HOLDS ONE BLACK DOT
WHICH STARTS TO GROW AND WILL ENGULF YOU

                                        then
there's always waking and I'm lying here
waiting for sunsets upside down to fade
the right way up, luring the real stars back.

Stone Circle

Fox-tracks on frost, the brook
less rowdy under films of ice

Between grey monoliths
logic has oozed away

We walk here, wonder, leave again

Shaggy cattle wander by
rubbing their flanks on uprights
lichen-smudged

In June the tiny yellow flowers
poke life up from thin soil

What happened here? A sacrifice?
Star-reverence?

No-one has ever found
a green sword buried
nor a skull in a stone box

An Open Letter to Librarians with Closed Minds

First, let's consider etymology.
Liber, a book. (That's Latin.) So we go
to libraries for books, not lattes, not
bright chats with friends. That's what cafés are for.
No library should be a social place.
True readers need their solitude enclosed
in hushed surroundings without clink of cups.

These days, like Goebbels and the Taleban,
you're getting rid of books you disapprove of.
'Because they clutter up the place! They're *so*
old-fashioned. No-one takes them out.' Ah, but
they may have been consulted many times
in situ, never stamped. No book you're there
to guard should ever be put up for sale
or jettisoned. Not ever. Who are you
to gauge what may or may not seem to be
important in the time to come? You should
be thinking not in weeks but centuries.
By putting keyboards where there should be books
you sabotage what you've been paid to do.
After a short while all technologies
must be replaced. So you build nothing up
when squandering funds you're given. A computer
is a convenience like a w.c.
or bus-stop – things unnoticed when not needed.
Each book stays outside time to form a new
kaleidoscope for every reader. They
explain the present to the future and
continually re-adjust the past
with facts, enchantment, fear, doubt or sheer fun.

Librarians must first of all love books –
the smell, the feel, the thrill to turn a page –
not systems or machines or fancy trends
bred in the gas of sociology.
They must protect what has been handed down,
resist bland politicians, vested interests,
insidious fifth-columnists bent on
destroying culture from within. If not,
you urge each generation to be more
illiterate, far less aware. You hold
the key to a choice of futures: one, a climb
to endless riches – one, a drab descent
to joylessness, aridity, the death
of breadth and challenge. It's for you to choose.

In the Small Hours

Curtains stirred. Mutter of thunder. Our dark-
gold tabby found crouching flat behind the sofa.

The west sky featureless. Electric clouds
smeared with quick yellow. Pause. Rumbling nearer.

Fetching a length of string I dangle it to tempt
a paw. He pats it listlessly, won't budge.

Fibres of light like gold nerves. Shorter silence.
Drumstammer. He steals away, belly scraping the carpet,

reaches a better haven beneath a chair. How
to explain. Console. As at the vet's. During

even that brief car-journey to the chalet
where we'd left him in good hands and flown off

to see orchids in Crete. My Welsh grandmother
feared thunder, stood by the french windows

with her four children each time there was a storm
feigning enjoyment till at last to her surprise

she felt no longer afraid. I jump when crash
seems simultaneous with double brilliance, kneel

by the wide-eyed cowerer to stroke his soft flank
getting rewarded by no purr. As well as all

the hullabaloo and flashing he must sense
a *wrongness* in the atmosphere, blaming no god,

no human, hoping for no end. Present misery
endures as constant. This morning's well-fed doze

was also endless, unremembered. In a life
unaware of future, where a past is just the best

route through a neighbour's rose-garden, some dreams
that make his limbs twitch and a set of blurry

warnings (largely unimportant), comparisons
between this state and that, because

impossible, convey no help. The first rain
clatters on the plastic awning. I recall

my sleeping wife upstairs and go round the house
dutifully shutting all the windows.

Light

for Lynn

Moonrise and the reddest flowers
turn silver.

        You pause before a mirror
where sunshine at two removes
provides synopsis of your beauty

        till daybreak . . .

      (yes, there's always
      possibility of candleshine
      or the flick for a sixty-
      watt bulb to shed false radiance
      but we'd surely plump for day
      as the true referee of light)

        . . . till dawn, then,
limns you with appropriate gold
conceding your loveliness
to colour, movement, wakefulness
and again my arms.

About the author

Harry Guest was born in Penarth in 1932. He read Modern Languages at Cambridge and taught in schools and universities in France, Japan and the UK before retiring in 1991.

His Collected Poems *A Puzzling Harvest* appeared from Anvil in 2002. Since 1994 he has been an Honorary Research Fellow of the University of Exeter. In 1998 he was awarded an Honorary Doctorate of Letters by the University of Plymouth. He was elected to Yr Academi Gymreig/The Welsh Academy in 2001. His poems have been translated into French, Japanese, Italian and Estonian. He is married to the historical novelist Lynn Guest and they have two children.